# LONDON *scene*

# The Spirit of London

No single book can attempt to do justice to the diversity of London, one of the greatest cities of the world. This publication gives the reader a tantalising glimpse of the fascinating places, people and traditions which combine to give the capital its unique appeal.

The Roman historian Tacitus gives us the first recorded detail of London, which even in the year AD 62 was a thriving market town, though not as large as many other Roman settlements. Towards the end of the Roman era London was enclosed by a wall, but little is known of its subsequent history until the reign of King Alfred, who refortified the city against the Danes. The arrival of the Normans brought a change in the fortunes of London, for William the Conqueror granted it a charter and began to build the Tower. Westminster Hall was begun by William Rufus and in 1176 the first London Bridge was built. From about 1190 until the fourteenth century the city was governed by the mayor and aldermen.

At the beginning of the fifteenth century, the period when the benevolent Dick Whittington was four times mayor, the plague first struck London and killed 30,000 people, but the city soon recovered and became extremely prosperous during the sixteenth century. Then in 1665 and 1666 two catastrophes occurred: the first was another epidemic of plague which killed 100,000 citizens, and the second was the Great Fire which destroyed practically the whole of the City, including St Paul's Cathedral. Most of London's finest buildings date from the second half of the seventeenth century onwards, and the greatest development of commerce took place in the nineteenth and present centuries.

During the Second World War London was bombed repeatedly and there was great destruction, but although three-quarters of all the houses in the capital suffered damage and a third of the city was destroyed, nothing could shake the Londoner's spirit. Today the scars have healed; new buildings have risen from the ruins and London once again greets her visitors with pride.

Nowhere is this pride more apparent than in the Chelsea Pensioners, retired servicemen who are cared for in the Royal Hospital at Chelsea. They wear a distinctive scarlet uniform, often adorned by hard-earned medals, and are among London's most delightful characters.

The London 'Bobby', as a policeman is affectionately called, is another familiar figure, his unenviable tasks including anything from directing the traffic to dealing with complex and dangerous situations. His knowledge of London is often encyclopaedic and he is consequently often approached by visitors seeking information or directions.

Pavement artists, street performers and market traders all add to the rich mosaic of London life. Some of the characters who were once a familiar part of the London scene have, alas, disappeared. The shoeblack is now seldom seen, and the lamplighter, with his tall pole, is only a memory; but others are still with us. The pearly 'kings and queens' who don their brilliant outfits on special occasions; the impassive commissionaires outside hotels, restaurants, cinemas and theatres; and the occasional city gent who sports his bowler hat and brolly. These, and many others, help to give London its unique personality.

The distinctive clock tower at the north end of the Houses of Parliament (**1** and **2**) is famous for the accuracy of its time-keeping. The hours are struck on its great bell, Big Ben, which was cast at the Whitechapel bell foundry in 1858.

# The City of London

The City of London was described as a 'busy emporium for trade and traders' as early as Roman times, and the description remains as true today as it did all those centuries ago. It is now a thriving financial and commercial centre which has within its square mile such famous institutions as the Bank of England, the Stock Exchange, the Royal Courts of Justice and Guildhall, as well as the headquarters of many international banks and insurance companies.

The City is administered as a separate unit and has its own Lord Mayor and Corporation as well as its own police force. The Lord Mayor of London officially resides at the Mansion House, a magnificent Palladian building designed by George Dance and constructed between 1739 and 1753, but the seat of the Corporation of London is Guildhall and it is here that the Mayor is elected. Part of Guildhall dates from 1411 but it was modified externally in the eighteenth century after being extensively damaged in the Great Fire. The Guildhall Library contains an unrivalled collection of books on all aspects of London.

Opposite the Mansion House stands the Bank of England, popularly known as 'The Old Lady of Threadneedle Street', where the nation's reserves of gold are stored. This famous bank was founded in 1694 but was moved here in 1734. It was nationalised in 1946 and has special responsibilities for issuing and printing banknotes – the security system is therefore very advanced!

The Stock Exchange, one of the world's centres of industrial finance, is nearby in Throgmorton Street.

The Royal Courts of Justice – the Law Courts – are situated in the Strand. There were originally twelve Inns of Court, but only four still exist in their traditional capacity as places where lawyers study for their bar examinations: Gray's Inn with its seventeenth-century gatehouse and magnificent sixteenth-century hall, Lincoln's Inn in Chancery Lane, and the Inner and Middle Temples of Fleet Street, the original headquarters of the Knights Templar. The Temple Church is one of only four surviving round churches in the country, built to imitate the Church of the Holy Sepulchre in Jerusalem.

The Central Criminal Court, popularly known as the Old Bailey, stands on the sight of Newgate Prison, which until the middle of the last century was the principal place of public execution in London. Many of the most famous trials of the century have been held here, including those of Crippen, Christie and Haig.

In complete contrast is one of the most beautiful landmarks of the capital – St Paul's Cathedral, Sir Christopher Wren's masterpiece. It was built of Portland stone between 1675 and 1710 to replace the thirteenth-century cathedral which had been destroyed by the Great Fire and it rises to 111 metres (365 feet) with a dome 34 metres (112 feet) in diameter, supported by twelve massive supports. This dome houses the famous Whispering Gallery and is decorated with paintings depicting the life of St Paul.

One of the newest City developments is at St Katharine Docks, where old warehouses have been beautifully restored to create a fascinating complex of shops, restaurants, hotels and marinas.

Visitors from across the world flock to see St Paul's Cathedral (3) in all its splendour, marvelling at the magnificent dome, which is the largest church dome in the world after St Peter's in Rome. The cathedral is one of London's most celebrated landmarks.

The interior of St Paul's Cathedral is as magnificent as the exterior. Outstanding carvings by Grinling Gibbons on the stalls and organ case in the quire (4) are complemented by Sir William Richmond's colourful mosaic on the ceiling, whilst a climb to the stone gallery of the dome gives visitors an unrivalled view of London (5). The cathedral is also the last resting place of many famous historic characters, including Admiral Lord Nelson (6), and the Duke of Wellington (7). Nearby is the Monument (8), built to commemorate the Great Fire and situated near where it started in Pudding Lane.

5

8

9

The ancient buildings of the City form a striking contrast to the new symbols of modern life, a contrast clearly illustrated by the dignified exterior of Guildhall (**9**) and the revolutionary design of Lloyd's of London (**10**). Historic buildings such as the Bank of England and the Royal Exchange stand near modern edifices like the National Westminster Bank Tower (**11**). Old and new are also brought together in the exciting new development of St Katharine Docks (**12**), where the old buildings constructed between 1824 and 1828 by Thomas Telford have been tastefully converted into modern shops and residences. The docks ceased to operate commercially in 1968.

13

The green and shady gardens of the Middle Temple (**13**) provide a tranquil oasis in the bustle of Fleet Street, whilst nearby the bronze sculpture of Justice, with her scale and sword, looks down from her lofty perch on the Old Bailey (**14**). The Royal Courts of Justice in the Strand (**15**) were built in the nineteenth century and opened by Queen Victoria in 1882. Two years later Tower Bridge (**16**) was erected having been designed by Sir Horace Jones and Sir John Wolfe Barry.

15

# The City of Westminster

The City of Westminster is one of the most historic areas in London as it contains both the seat of Government and the crowning place of kings and queens. The Houses of Parliament and Westminster Abbey face each other across Parliament Square, where statues of Sir Winston Churchill, Abraham Lincoln, Disraeli and several other statesmen stand. To the north of Westminster Abbey stands St Margaret's, a fashionable church for weddings since the seventeenth century. Samuel Pepys, John Milton and Sir Winston Churchill were all married there and it is also the burial place of Sir Walter Raleigh.

The present Houses of Parliament were completed in 1865 on the site of the old Palace of Westminster, the principal residence of the monarch between the reigns of Edward the Confessor and Henry VIII. Most of the old palace was destroyed in a fire in 1834, but fortunately the magnificent Westminster Hall, which had been built between 1097 and 1099 by William Rufus, survived. The hammerbeam roof of the hall is the earliest and largest of its kind in existence, having been constructed between 1394 and 1401, and the hall itself was the traditional venue for the lying in state of monarchs.

The two principal chambers of the Houses of Parliament – the House of Commons and the House of Lords – are set either side of a central hall and corridor. The present House of Commons is new, as its predecessor was destroyed by enemy action in 1941, and at its entrance stands the Churchill Arch, constructed from stone salvaged from the original structure. The House of Lords is an ornately furnished chamber with red leather peers' benches and the woolsack, the traditional seat of the Lord Chancellor. Behind this is the throne from which the Queen ceremonially opens each session of Parliament.

The clock tower, almost 98 metres (320 feet) high, contains Big Ben, the hour bell weighing more than 13 tonnes. The four clock faces each have a diameter of more than 6 metres (22 feet).

A church has stood on the current site of Westminster Abbey since Saxon times, but the abbey itself was founded by Edward the Confessor in 1050 as a Benedictine monastery and made the crowning place of English sovereigns: since William the Conqueror all coronations except those of Edward V and Edward VIII have taken place here. The rebuilding of the abbey was begun by Henry III between 1216 and 1272 and between 1503 and 1519 Henry VII added the chapel to the eastern end. The towers, which are almost 69 metres (225 feet) high, were added in the mid eighteenth century by Nicholas Hawksmoor.

Many English sovereigns, politicians, poets, scientists and other well-known people are buried or remembered in the abbey, and it is also the site of the tomb of the Unknown Warrior, as well as the Coronation Chair and the Stone of Scone, on which the Scottish kings were once crowned.

Westminster Cathedral is the largest and most important Roman Catholic church in England. Although its architecture is Early Byzantine in style, it is nevertheless relatively modern, having been begun in 1895 and consecrated in 1910. The interior is embellished with striking marble and mosaics, whilst externally the most prominent feature is the campanile, which is 83 metres (273 feet) high and is surmounted by a cross 3 metres (11 feet) high.

The Houses of Parliament (17) rise in Gothic splendour on the banks of the Thames. A light shining from the clock tower by night and the Union Flag flying on top of the Victoria Tower by day indicate that the House of Commons is sitting.

18      The House of Lords (**18**) is a magnificently colourful chamber where lively debates take place between Church of England bishops and archbishops, and peers who have inherited titles or who have been appointed for life. The State Opening of Parliament takes place here, with the Queen reading from the throne in the centre and the Lord Chancellor seated on the woolsack (**20**). In the House of Commons (**19**) the Speaker presides, whilst the Prime Minister and his ministers sit on the front bench on the right side, facing the Opposition on the left side. When voting, Members give their names at desks in one of the Division Lobbies (**21**).

19

20

21

22

Viewed from the south the true
splendour of the Houses of
Parliament can be appreciated (22),
with the River Thames flowing
timelessly by in the foreground.
Forming an equally dramatic
intrusion into London's skyline, the
famous twin towers of Westminster
Abbey (24) rise majestically skywards, as does the single red and
grey striped campanile of
Westminster Cathedral (23), the
principal Roman Catholic church in
England. More than a hundred
different kinds of marble from
across the world were used to
decorate the interior of Westminster
Cathedral and there are chapels to
commemorate the saints of England,
Ireland and Scotland.

23

2

25

27

The interior of Westminister Abbey is a veritable house of British history. Henry VII is commemorated in the Henry VII Chapel, which has unusual circular vaulting on the ceiling, intricate tracery and rich carving (**28**). His tomb is a remarkably elaborate resting place, with Torrigiani cherubs supporting the King's Arms which are surrounded by the Garter (**25**). The gilded bronze effigy of Eleanor of Castile, wife of Edward I, is equally attractive (**27**) whilst the tomb of the Unknown Warrior (**26**) is a poignant reminder of all those who sacrificed their lives in the First World War.

# London's Pageantry

Despite London's prominent position in the fast-moving modern world, the capital has managed to retain an enormous number of traditional ceremonies which bring colour and pageantry to the capital. Many of these ceremonies involve troops which were originally required to protect the Crown, but which now have the happier task of enthralling the millions of visitors who come to watch them every year. Pageantry takes many forms and, apart from infrequent elaborate events such as royal weddings and coronations, there are daily ceremonies to be seen in various parts of the capital. At Buckingham Palace and St James's Palace, and in Whitehall, guard-mounting is carried out every day.

Units of the Household Division are normally stationed in or around London. The Division consists of the Life Guards, the Blues and Royals and the five regiments of Foot Guards: Grenadier, Coldstream, Welsh, Irish and Scots Guards. The magnificent horses and accoutrements of the Life Guards and the Blues and Royals are a constant source of wonder, but it is the Household Cavalry, the mounted regiment, which provides the Queen's lifeguard.

Between Whitehall and St James's Park lies Horse Guards, once part of the royal palace of Whitehall, now no longer standing. The Changing of the Mounted Guard in the forecourt of the former palace is one of the most popular daily London ceremonies. Nearby Horse Guards Parade is the venue for another exciting and colourful pageant – Trooping the Colour – which takes place annually in June on the Queen's official birthday. This is probably the most spectacular military display in the country, dating back more than 200 years but with its roots probably stretching back to medieval times. The Queen rides in an open carriage from Buckingham Palace, wearing the uniform of one of the regiments of which she is Colonel-in-Chief, to Horse Guards Parade, where the Brigade of Guards and the Household Cavalry await her. Her Majesty takes the salute and a marvellous display of 'trooping', or carrying, of the colours of selected regiments then follows. The Queen is then escorted by her Guards into The Mall and back to Buckingham Palace.

The King's Troop, Royal Artillery, also plays an important part in royal and state ceremonies, as it is this troop which fires the traditional 41-gun salute at midday in Hyde Park on such occasions as the Queen's Accession Day (February 6), the Queen's birthday (April 21), Coronation Day (June 2), the Duke of Edinburgh's birthday (June 10) and the Queen Mother's birthday (August 4). On the same days, a 62-gun salute is fired at the Tower of London by the Honourable Artillery Company.

The Ceremony of the Keys at the Tower of London is steeped in history: every evening for 700 years the main gate of the Tower has been locked by the Chief Yeoman Warder and an escort of Guards in this colourful ritual.

London has many other brilliantly colourful events, like the dazzling displays at the Lord Mayor's Show when the new Lord Mayor rides to the Royal Courts of Justice in an eighteenth-century coach with a bodyguard of Pikemen and Musketeers – a ceremony which is at least 600 years old. From the traditional occasions, like the distribution of Royal maundy money, and swan-upping on the Thames, to the spectacle of the Notting Hill Carnival and the University Boat Race, London has many colourful events to offer throughout the year.

The splendid, highly polished uniforms and massive horses of the Mounted Guard in the forecourt of Horse Guards – here a trooper of the Blues and Royals (**29**) – must be one of London's most colourful and awe-inspiring sights.

The colour and splendour of London's pageantry is enhanced by the uniforms of the five regiments of Foot Guards (30) – from left to right, Coldstream, Irish, Scots, Welsh and Grenadier. The Massed Bands and other regiments which take part in Trooping the Colour (31 and 34) make this a most memorable spectacle, whilst the sight of the Household Cavalry filling The Mall (32) is a scene which cannot be matched anywhere else in the world. The procession of the Lord Mayor's Show moves from Guildhall, pausing at St Paul's Cathedral, where the Lord Mayor is presented with a Bible by the Dean and Chapter (33), before continuing down Fleet Street to the Royal Courts of Justice.

33

34

The Life Guards (**35**) perform a vital part in many of the ceremonies which take place in London and
Her Majesty The Queen is present at many of the most colourful pageants. Every year the Queen attends
the State Opening of Parliament, travelling the distance between Buckingham Palace and the Palace of
Westminster in the Irish State Coach, watched by many thousands of onlookers who line the route (**36**).
The traditional ceremony continues once the Queen reaches Westminster, for she must sit enthroned in
the Lords while the Prime Minister and the Cabinet are summoned from the Commons.

37

38

39

The ceremony of Changing the Guard at Buckingham Palace (**37**) takes place in the forecourt every morning during the summer and on alternate mornings from mid-August to mid-April. Horse Guards (**41**) off Whitehall is another place where Changing the Guard attracts fascinated onlookers. Two mounted troopers (**40**) are posted there daily. Horse Guards Parade is the square parade ground where Trooping the Colour takes place every June. The Honourable Artillery Company fires a salute at the Tower of London (**38**) only on special occasions, but the Ceremony of the Keys at the Tower of London (**39**) takes place every evening.

41

# Museums and Galleries

London's galleries and museums contain some of the world's finest treasures and an unrivalled selection of interesting exhibitions. The largest collection in London, and indeed one of the largest in the world, is contained within the British Museum, which was founded in 1753 and which shows the works of man from all over the world from prehistoric to comparatively modern times. Perhaps its most famous possessions, however, are the Elgin Marbles, from temples in Athens, and the Rosetta Stone, which was used by scholars to find the key to deciphering Egyptian hieroglyphs. British treasures include the beautiful seventh-century Sutton Hoo finds and the twelfth-century Lewis chessmen.

The Victoria and Albert Museum is equally impressive, with an outstanding collection of fine and applied arts housed in a grand building opened in 1909 by Edward VII and situated in Cromwell Road. Just next door, and especially popular with children, is the Natural History Museum. Within this vast and elegant building, unsuspecting visitors may come face to face with anything from a huge dinosaur to working displays of their own insides! The Science Museum is just as interesting, with a collection covering subjects as diverse as agriculture and telecommunications. Always popular with youngsters is an exciting 'hands-on' exhibition which introduces children to basic scientific principles.

The Geological Museum is the national museum of earth sciences and, as such, displays a wonderful collection of fossils, gemstones and examples of every kind of geological formation. A piece of the moon can even be seen here! Firmly back on earth, however, is the Museum of London, which is devoted entirely to the capital and its people, from prehistoric times to the present day.

The Museum of Mankind has a more international flavour, and the Commonwealth Institute in Kensington High Street is a 'living museum' which introduces the visitor to life in the countries of the Commonwealth.

Other popular museums include the Imperial War Museum, which illustrates all aspects of the World Wars and other military operations involving Britain and the Commonwealth since 1914. The Cabinet War Rooms in King Charles Street provided accommodation to protect Sir Winston Churchill during the Second World War and are open to the public, whilst the London Dungeon, the Guinness World of Records, Madame Tussaud's and the Bethnal Green Museum of Childhood provide lighter entertainment for visitors.

London is equally rich in art galleries, from the National Gallery in Trafalgar Square, which houses one of the world's finest collections of European art, to the smaller galleries, such as the Wallace Collection in Manchester Square, with its unrivalled representation of eighteenth-century French art. The Tate Gallery houses the national collection of British painting, modern foreign painting and modern sculpture, and the Courtauld Institute is largely devoted to works by the French Impressionists. Mention must be made too of the Royal Academy in Piccadilly and its famous Summer Exhibition of contemporary art, and the National Portrait Gallery with its fine collection of portraits spanning six centuries.

The noble exterior of the Natural History Museum (**42**) in South Kensington is a sight worth viewing in its own right, but the collection housed within its walls would take many days to explore fully. The museum was opened in 1881 as an offshoot of the British Museum.

43

44

The British Museum's imposing columns (**43**) provide a fitting entrance to the myriad treasures contained within its many rooms and galleries. The collection of Roman and Greek antiquities is among the best in the world. Madame Tussaud's (**44**), the famous waxworks museum, has been one of London's greatest attractions for more than 150 years. The Science Museum (**45**), a favourite with children, contains remarkable collections of machinery, medical equipment and scientific apparatus, including equipment used for space travel and man's trips to the moon. The Royal Academy of Arts (**46**) houses permanent collections throughout the year, as well as being home to the famous Summer Exhibition of contemporary art. The Tate Gallery (**47**) is celebrated for its collection of modern British art, dating from 1850.

45

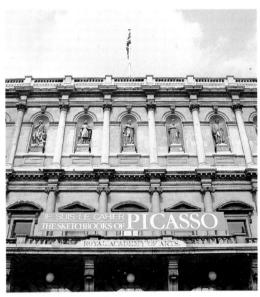

46

47

The paintings in the National Gallery (**48**) include a representative selection of masterpieces from every major European school. Next door, the National Portrait Gallery displays paintings of important people in British history from Tudor times to the present day, including this portrait of the Brontë sisters (**49**) by their brother. HMS *Belfast* (**50**), moored near Tower Bridge, is the unusual setting for part of the Imperial War Museum Collection. The National Maritime Museum at Greenwich (**51**) contains a wide range of relics from this seafaring nation. The Dickens House Museum (**52**), home of the novelist between 1837 and 1839, now contains the most comprehensive Dickens library in the world plus many other interesting artefacts.

**48**

**49**

# Royal Landmarks

London has been the home of the British Royal Family for centuries, and although many former palaces have now been converted for other uses, some still remain as royal residences. The most famous of these is surely Buckingham Palace.

The palace takes its name from Buckingham House, which was built in 1703 as the home of the Duke of Buckingham and subsequently bought by George III in 1762. It was remodelled by Nash in 1825 and has been the home of the monarch since Queen Victoria came to the throne. The east wing, which is the side the public sees, was added in 1847. Today the Queen lives at the palace for only part of the year and when she is in residence the Royal Standard is flown. The huge marble statue outside the palace at the head of The Mall depicts Queen Victoria surrounded by figures of Justice, Truth and Motherhood, and surmounted by Courage, Constancy and the winged figure of Victory.

The main palace is now open to the public at certain times, and items from the Royal Collection can be seen at the nearby Queen's Gallery which was originally designed as a conservatory by John Nash. The Royal Mews is also open to the public at certain times and an interesting selection of royal transport can be seen there, including the magnificent State Coach, used for coronations, and the glass coach, used for royal weddings.

The oldest of all the royal residences in London, although no longer inhabited by the Royal Family, is the Tower of London. Begun by William the Conqueror in 1078, this famous fortress was enlarged several times in later years. Throughout its long history it has been put to many uses including that of a zoo, the Royal Mint, the first Royal Observatory and now as a museum to house the national collection of armour and the Crown Jewels. It is perhaps most famous for being a prison, however, and such diverse characters as Lady Jane Grey and Rudolph Hess were held captive in the Yeoman Gaoler's House at various times. Indeed, heroes and traitors from centuries of British history have been incarcerated in this grim fortress, often to lose their heads on the block or to be hung from the gallows.

The Yeomen of the Guard – or Beefeaters – were originally formed to be a bodyguard for Henry VII, after the Battle of Bosworth in 1485. They still wear the Tudor uniform chosen by the King, and now give guided tours of the Tower. The ravens which roost there stay by courtesy of a legend which claims that the old Empire would crumble if they left!

Kensington Palace and St James's Palace are also to be found in the capital. Queen Victoria was born and brought up at Kensington Palace, a delightful building which was acquired by William III in 1689 and remodelled by Sir Christopher Wren. Although it remains a royal residence, the State Apartments and the Court Dress Collection are open to visitors. St James's Palace was long the official London residence of the sovereign. George III was the last monarch to live here; the palace is now occupied by the Prince of Wales's Household and is therefore not open. Many sovereigns were born here, including Charles II, James II, Mary II, Queen Anne and George IV, and several royal marriages have been solemnised here.

Gaily coloured sailing-boats moored on the banks of the Thames near Traitors' Gate, the river entry to the Tower of London (**53**), form a stark contrast to the grim reception which must have greeted prisoners throughout the Tower's long history.

The vividly coloured costume of the Yeoman Warders or Beefeaters (54) at the Tower of London is a favourite photographic subject for the millions of tourists who visit the capital each year. The specially selected ex-servicemen also now give guided tours of the Tower, delighting in relating some of the many stories which are associated with their place of work. The key position the Tower occupies on the Thames can clearly be seen in this view from Tower Bridge (55). Although the Tower is the oldest royal residence in London, it is Buckingham Palace (56) which is today identified as the home of the Royal Family. The Queen and Duke of Edinburgh have private suites in the north wing overlooking Green Park, but it is the dignified east façade which most visitors see and admire. Many people are privileged to pass through the gates of this famous palace in order to attend one of the summer garden parties, or to receive recognition for their achievements.

The Queen Victoria Memorial (**57**) stands outside Buckingham Palace and was unveiled by George V in 1911. Nearby, in the Royal Mews (**60**), an interesting collection of royal transport is on view to the public. Clarence House (**61**) is now the home of the Queen Mother, whilst Hampton Court Palace (**58**) is no longer a royal residence, despite having been a royal favourite for more than 200 years. The Royal Naval College at Greenwich (**59**) is built on the site of a former royal palace called Placentia, which was the favourite home of the Tudor kings.

62

63

The Queen and the Duke of Edinburgh (**62**) travelling to the State Opening of Parliament in 1992.
The Queen, the Duke of Edinburgh, the Duke of Kent (behind) and the Prince of Wales (**63**) on the
balcony of Buckingham Palace on the occasion of the Trooping of the Colour in 1993.

64

65

St James's Palace (**64**) is an irregular building created by Henry VIII, and parts of it survive from the sixteenth century, including the Chapel Royal. The Palace is occupied by the Prince of Wales's Household. Sentries of the Grenadier Guards stand at the gates (**65**). The Prince of Wales has apartments at Kensington Palace (**66**), but its first royal resident was William III, whose statue can be seen beyond the gates. When he bought it in 1689, the palace was situated in the village of Kensington.

# Green London

One of the special joys of London is the amount of space devoted to parks, gardens, squares and open areas, providing peaceful oases in the midst of all the buildings and traffic.

Hyde Park merges with Kensington Gardens, but there is a marked difference between the two parks, even though they were once one and the same place: before Henry VIII enclosed Hyde Park as a hunting-chase, the area was a vast area of countryside. Since then it has had a varied history, having been used for horse-racing, duelling, as the site for the 1851 Great Exhibition and as a defensive camp during the Second World War. Today it is a peaceful park, with the Serpentine forming a wonderful habitat for wild creatures and for sailing, boating and swimming. In the north-east corner of the park is Speakers' Corner, where anyone can stand up and talk on any subject they please.

Kensington Gardens were once the private gardens of Kensington Palace, but they now form a delightful refuge from the hurried pace of life beyond their boundaries. In the children's playground carved pixies frolic alongside a statue of Peter Pan and in the Serpentine Gallery there are monthly exhibitions of contemporary art.

Regent's Park was also once part of Henry VIII's hunting-forest, but in 1812 it was transformed into its present design by Nash under the direction of the Prince Regent – hence its name. Today excellent performances are put on at the open-air theatre and there are facilities for archery, tennis and sailing.

St James's Park and Green Park stand on either side of The Mall, the former in fact occupying a site where a hospital for lepers once stood amid marshy surroundings. Today nothing could be more relaxing and peaceful than a stroll through St James's Park, thanks to the efforts of Henry VIII, who converted the area into a deer park. Contributions by Charles II and George IV, who designed the formal gardens and the lovely lake, enhanced the natural beauty of the park. Green Park, as its name suggests, is mainly laid to lawn, and was once the favourite walking-place of Charles II, who took his constitutional stroll here – hence Constitution Hill.

Further west, Hampton Court, Bushy Park and Richmond Park provide just some of the delightful green and floral areas available in London. Hampton Court has an outstanding array of formal gardens and a famous maze, whilst nearby Bushy Park provides a delightfully informal contrast, with its atmosphere of the natural countryside. Richmond Park comprises 1,002 hectares (2,500 acres) where red and fallow deer roam and exotic shrubs coexist with wild flowers. Further west still are the Royal Botanic Gardens at Kew, badly damaged by the hurricane-force winds of October 1987, but still providing 121 hectares (300 acres) of exotic plants and trees from all over the world. Across the Thames from here is Syon Park, the country's first national gardening-centre.

Other green tracts in London include the 324 hectares (800 acres) of Hampstead Heath, the deer-park and children's facilities of Battersea Park, the magnificent Wren buildings of Greenwich Park and the wonderful peacocks of Holland Park, once the garden of a private house.

A riot of floral colour fills Queen Mary's Gardens in Regent's Park (**67**), making it the ideal place for quiet contemplation or a relaxing stroll. It is hard to believe that this was once part of a huge hunting forest, such is the beauty of the formal gardens here.

68

A carpet of daffodils forms a delightful springtime scene in Kensington Gardens (**68**), another of London's green oases. In the distance can be seen the Albert Memorial, which was erected as a monument to Queen Victoria's consort in 1863-76 and was designed by Sir George Gilbert Scott. The Long Water and the Serpentine (**69**) separate Kensington Gardens from Hyde Park and prove the ideal spot for water activities as well as for local wildlife. Speakers' Corner (**70**) acts as a forum for free speech, and various orators use it to proclaim their opinions on public, religious and political issues.

69

70

London's open spaces are popular
recreational areas. Both Hampstead
Heath (**71**) and Green Park (**72**) offer
interesting areas in which to walk or
just to watch the world go by.
St James's Park (**73**) is equally popular
with residents and visitors alike, its lake
providing added attraction, as does the
lake at Crystal Palace Park (**75**) with its
many wildfowl waiting for titbits from
passing promenaders. The Royal
Botanic Gardens at Kew are fascinating
for gardening enthusiasts and contain
the new, technically advanced Princess
of Wales Conservatory (**74**), which is
able to support a great variety of plants
at different temperatures.

73

75

# The Sights of London

Most visitors will wish to see something of the historic thoroughfares of London, and there is no better starting-place than Buckingham Palace, from where the broad tree-lined Mall leads to Trafalgar Square. At the end of The Mall and adjoining the Admiralty, of which it forms a part, stands the impressively proportioned Admiralty Arch, designed by Sir Aston Webb and completed in 1911.

Trafalgar Square, named in commemoration of Nelson's great naval victory of 1805, is dominated by Nelson's Column, which rises high above the square, giving the famous pigeons a lofty perch. On its pedestal are four bronze reliefs cast from captured French cannon, representing scenes from the battles of St Vincent, the Nile, Copenhagen and Trafalgar. The bronze lions at the corners of the pedestals are the work of Landseer.

From Trafalgar Square it is only a short way to Piccadilly Circus, one of the busiest junctions in the West End of London. Beneath the roadway lies one of the main interchange stations of London's underground railway network. The well-known statue of Eros, a memorial to one of London's greatest philanthropists, the 7th Earl of Shaftesbury, can be seen in Piccadilly Circus.

The broad highway of Whitehall, leading from Trafalgar Square to the Houses of Parliament at Westminster, is flanked by many large administrative buildings. Its name perpetuates the former Palace of Whitehall which stood here until the eighteenth century and which was the principal centre of London court life in Tudor and Stuart times. Of the palace, where Henry VIII died and where Elizabeth I entertained, there remains only the Banqueting Hall. In the centre of Whitehall stands the Cenotaph, designed by Sir Edwin Lutyens as a memorial to the fallen of both World Wars.

Downing Street, a turning off Whitehall, is the official residence of both the Prime Minister, at number 10, and the Chancellor of the Exchequer, at number 11.

One of London's tallest buildings is the Telecom Tower which rises to 189 metres (619 feet) and was opened in May 1966.

An equally famous landmark is the Royal Albert Hall, a large circular amphitheatre covered by a glass dome, which can accommodate 10,000 people and which is the venue for the annual Henry Wood Promenade Concerts, held from July to September. Opposite the hall, in Kensington Gardens, is the Albert Memorial, depicting Prince Albert reading a catalogue of the Great Exhibition of 1851, for which he was largely responsible.

Marble Arch, a triumphal arch modelled by John Nash on the Arch of Constantine in Rome, originally stood in front of Buckingham Palace, but was moved to its present site in 1850. Indeed the designs of John Nash can be found throughout London, as can those of Sir Christopher Wren, who was responsible for the architecture of many of the city's churches, including St Michael-at-Cornhill, St Bride's of Fleet Street (internationally known as the 'parish church of the press'), and St Mary-le-Bow, Cheapside, with its lofty spire crowned by a dragon weathervane 3 metres (9 feet) high, and its famous Bow Bells, within whose earshot true Cockneys are said to be born.

The Christmas tree illuminated in Trafalgar Square (**76**), with the classical-style church of St Martin-in-the-Fields, the masterpiece of James Gibbs, in the background. The tree is an annual gift from the people of Norway.

77

78

80

The Mall has been the route for many historic processions and is lined with fine buildings, such as those which constitute Nash Terraces (**77**). At the end of the tree-lined Mall, which was first laid out in about 1660, is Admiralty Arch (**80**), part of the Admiralty. In the centre of nearby Whitehall stands the Cenotaph (**78**), the memorial to the fallen of both World Wars, and in Downing Street, a turning off Whitehall, is the official residence of the Prime Minister at number 10 (**79**). The façade of this unimposing building hides a large and impressive interior where many important guests have been received. The Albert Memorial (**81**) in Kensington Gardens, opposite the Albert Hall, was unveiled in 1876.

81

84

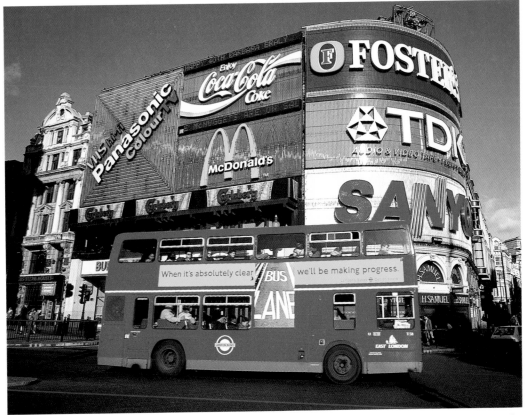

85

The activity of Piccadilly Circus (**82** and **85**) is surveyed by Eros, an aluminium sculpture, which is properly entitled the Shaftesbury Memorial, as a tribute to the Earl of Shaftesbury. The Circus is a popular meeting-place and is particularly interesting at night when the advertising hoardings light up the sky in a constantly changing kaleidoscope of colour. Marble Arch (**83**) marks the north-east corner of Hyde Park and is situated near Speakers' Corner. Hyde Park Corner, at the far end of Park Lane, has another arch – Constitution Arch (**84**) – which dates from the 1820s and was originally known as Wellington Arch.

86

88

The sights of London are many and varied: from the Gothic splendour of Southwark Cathedral (86), which contains a chapel to the memory of John Harvard, the first benefactor of the American university, to the modern silhouette of Telecom Tower (87), which is one of London's tallest buildings. Canary Wharf (88), to the east, is a spectacular 1980s riverside office development. Cleopatra's Needle (89) also rises skywards, an obelisk of pink granite which in fact has no connection with Cleopatra at all. It was originally erected in about 1500 BC in Egypt, but was presented to Britain in 1819. The illuminated dome and spires of St Paul's Cathedral (90) dominate the skyline above Blackfriars Bridge. The new Thames Barrier (91) has also become a tourist attraction, although its primary function is to prevent serious flooding in London.

89

# Shops and Entertainment

While there is much of historic and cultural interest in London, it is also pleasant to spend time browsing in the many fine shops, department stores and lively markets. In the evenings the city has much to offer by way of entertainment, ranging from theatrical performances to night clubs, opera and ballet.

Perhaps the most famous shopping street of all is Oxford Street, stretching as it does for more than a mile from Marble Arch to Tottenham Court Road. Shops of every description line either side of this busy thoroughfare and many of the country's chain stores have their largest shops here. Crossing Oxford Street at Oxford Circus is Regent Street, with its fine selection of elegant clothes shops for both men and women. The street itself was laid out by John Nash between 1813 and 1820, but it was completely rebuilt in 1900.

Piccadilly is home to numerous airlines and travel shops as well as an impressive range of food, clothes and bookshops. The nearby Trocadero Centre also contains a number of interesting shops and restaurants. Burlington Arcade, off Piccadilly, has some of the most elegant small shops in London, whilst nearby Bond Street is known for its top-quality goods, and leading names in fashion, jewellery and cosmetics stand side by side with art dealers.

Harrods, in Knightsbridge, claims to be the largest department store in Europe and it is flanked by equally luxurious fashion shops and antique dealers.

Jermyn Street and Savile Row are both famous for their high-class tailoring establishments, whilst the King's Road contains a fascinating selection of fashionable shops.

Street markets are still an important part of London's commercial life, and the atmosphere created by the traders and enthusiastic bargain-hunters is exciting. Fruit and vegetables dominate the Berwick Street Market, which is open daily except Sundays, whilst Brixton Market is renowned for its Caribbean produce. Camden Lock Market and Camden Passage offer a rich and varied mixture of antiques and bric-à-brac, whilst those wishing to find a true Cockney atmosphere should head towards Middlesex Street, which is home to the famous Petticoat Lane Market. The street acquired its popular name in the seventeenth century, because of the number of clothes dealers who congregated there.

Portobello Road Market also has a wonderful atmosphere, with more than 2,000 stalls and shops containing all kinds of furniture, clothes, coins and collectors' items, and numerous buskers and street performers entertaining the crowds. Covent Garden, former site of the famous fruit and vegetable market, north of the Strand, has been extensively restored and is now a lively shopping area, with wine bars, restaurants and theatres and an open Piazza and covered Central Market.

London's entertainment scene is equally colourful and diverse. All tastes are catered for in theatre, music and dance, and London's West End exports many of its finest productions to the rest of the world. Whether classical music, Shakespearian theatre, raucous comedy or discotheques are your preference, London has something for everyone.

Harrods (**92**), one of the world's best-known department stores, started life as a small grocery shop set up by C.D. Harrod in 1861. Today the name is synonymous with quality and the shop's illuminated façade is one of London's best-loved landmarks, particularly at Christmas-time.

93

94

95

Travellers from all over the world shop at Harrods (**93**) drawn by the variety and quality of the items on display. At sales times, queues often form several days in advance of the opening, knowing that the wait will be worthwhile in terms of money saved. The shops of Bond Street (**94**) are also very popular for their high-quality goods and antiques, whilst Selfridges in Oxford Street (**95**) is another store which has become a landmark in its own right and which also attracts customers from across the world.

The characters and produce of London's
markets rival each other only in colour. From
the stalls of Shepherd Market (**96**) to the
marvellous displays at the Berwick Street
Market in Soho (**99**), there is always a
bargain available. Once a famous flower
market, Covent Garden (**98**) has now
become a favourite meeting-place for many
Londoners. King's Road, Chelsea (**97**), is the
place frequented by young people looking
for modern clothes. At the other end of the
scale, Sotheby's (**100**), the international fine
art auctioneers, was founded in 1744 but
moved to the present salerooms in New
Bond Street just before the First World War.

98

99

100

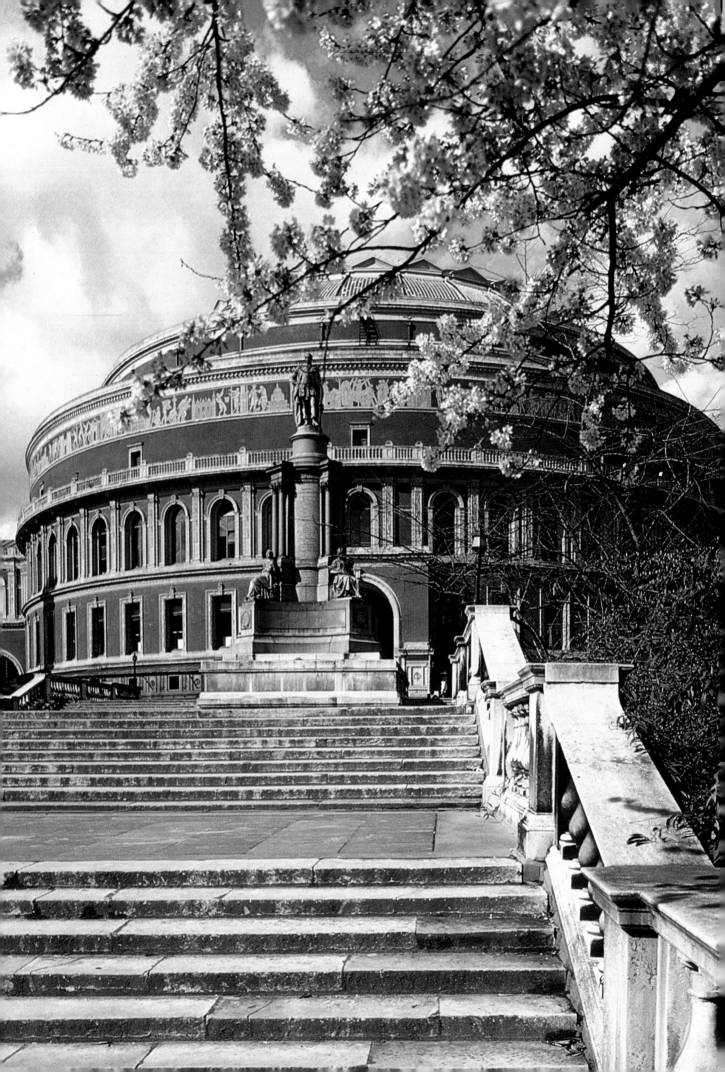

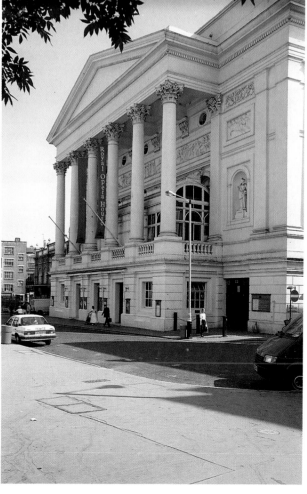

The capital's entertainment scene is as varied as it is prestigious. The famous Promenade Concerts of the Albert Hall (**101**), the varied orchestral and ballet performances which take place at the Royal Festival Hall (**103**) on the South Bank (**102**) and the marvellous operas and ballets which are performed at the Royal Opera House or the Theatre Royal, Covent Garden, as it is known (**104**), are just some of the many cultural events available.

**105**

The Barbican Centre (**105**) is the largest arts complex in Europe, where a wide range of performing arts is presented to an ever-appreciative audience. It was officially opened in March 1982 by Her Majesty The Queen and is maintained by the City of London. The Barbican is the London base of the Royal Shakespeare Company, whose worldwide reputation attracts record-breaking attendances. There are also several restaurants in the complex, one of which overlooks the artificial lake.

**Acknowledgements**
The publishers are grateful to the following for permission to reproduce photographs: Madame Tussaud's, London (**44**); Science Museum (**45**); National Portrait Gallery (**49**); Dean and Chapter of Westminster Abbey (**25, 26, 27, 28**); Dean and Chapter of St Paul's Cathedral (**4, 6, 7**); Tim Graham (**62, 63**); Sotheby's (**100**); British Tourist Authority (**37, 103**); Crown Copyright, reproduced by permission of the Controller of Her Majesty's Stationery Office (**39**).